A Ladybird Bible Book

Peter

Text by Jenny Robertson
Illustrations by Alan Parry

Scripture Union/Ladybird

Jesus had died and come to life again. For many weeks his friends saw him, talked with him and ate with him. Then the time came for him to go back to Heaven to be with God. He promised to send his friends a special helper, God's Holy

Spirit, who would give them the power to do all God wanted.

On the morning of the festival of Pentecost the friends met as usual. Suddenly the roar of a rushing wind filled the room. Leaping flames touched their heads and they felt that God was specially close to them. Excitedly they praised God, and at once they found themselves speaking in different languages. Still praising God they ran out into the street.

The sound of their laughter and happy shouts soon drew a crowd. People from many foreign countries had come to Jerusalem for the festival. They were amazed to hear Jesus' friends talk about God in languages they all understood. Some people tried to turn it into a joke. 'These men are drunk!' they jeered. 'No!' Peter declared, and he explained to them about Jesus: 'You put God's Son to death here in Jerusalem, but God brought him back to life, just as he said he would. Now if you believe in him you must stop doing wrong. Then be baptised in the name of Jesus and God will forgive you. He will give you his Holy Spirit to help you do the things that please him.'

'We must do what Peter says!' many agreed. About three thousand people joined Jesus' friends that day. They listened eagerly as Peter and the others told them more about Jesus.

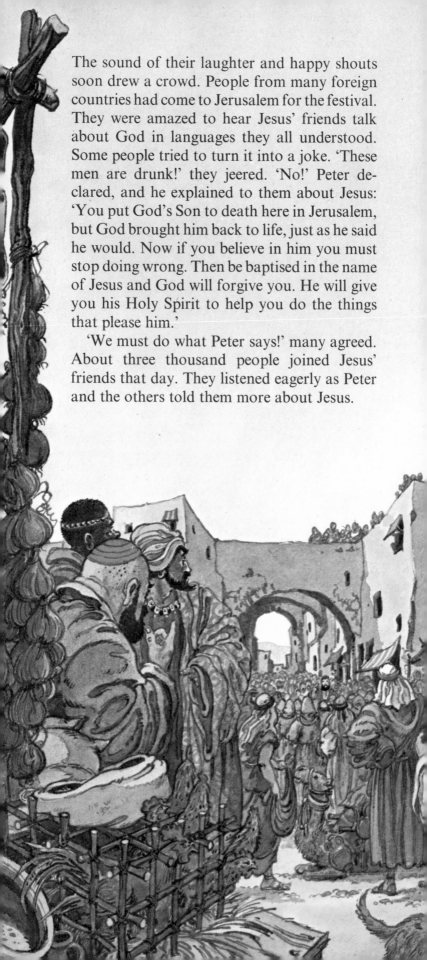

The new followers of Jesus shared everything they had. They met in one another's houses to share meals and pray together. Every day they went to the Temple to praise God, and were so full of joy that more and more people kept joining their group.

Once, on their way to pray in the Temple, Peter and his friend John met a lame beggar. He used to sit beside one of the gates all day, calling: 'Give me some money! I've never walked in all my life. Give me a coin to buy food!'

Peter and John stopped, and the beggar watched them hopefully. 'I have no money to give you,' Peter said, 'But I shall give you what I have. In the name of Jesus I command you; get up and walk!' He helped the beggar to his feet. At once the man felt strength flow into his weak ankles. He let go of Peter's hand and started to walk. Soon he was jumping and leaping in the air, shouting: 'Look, I can walk. I can really move about. How good God is! Thank you, God! Now at last I can walk like everyone else after being lame all my life.' He ran into the Temple where everyone was amazed to see him walking about, praising God.

Peter explained that it was the power of Jesus which cured the lame man. This made the priests angry. They thought they had got rid of Jesus! They arrested Peter and John and warned them to stop talking about Jesus, but the friends took no notice. Soon they were arrested again.

'We told you not to teach about Jesus,' the High Priest said, but Peter answered boldly, 'We must do what God wants. He brought Jesus back to life and we must tell people about him.' When the priests heard this, they wanted to put Peter and his friends to death, but a wise teacher called Gamaliel advised them to be careful. 'If this new faith is not from God it will fade away and be forgotten. But if it is from God nothing you can do will stop it. Be careful! You might find yourselves fighting against God!'

So the priests had Peter and John beaten and then set them free. The friends were glad God had let them suffer for the sake of Jesus. They took no notice of the priests, but kept on telling everyone about Jesus.

It was no longer safe to be a follower of Jesus. Believers were dragged off to prison and punished. Many of them were forced to leave Jerusalem. Wherever they went they told people about Jesus, and the new faith spread everywhere.

One man, called Philip, went to Samaria. Everyone gathered round to hear about Jesus. Lame people walked again. Evil spirits were driven away.

Philip baptised everyone who wanted to follow Jesus. There were so many new believers that Peter and John came from Jerusalem to meet them. When Peter and John prayed for them they received the Holy Spirit, too. He would give them new power to help them serve God.

At about that time a very important man was travelling home from Jerusalem. He was the Queen of Ethiopia's treasurer, a man who loved God and wanted to learn more about him. God guided Philip to him. Philip ran up to his chariot and began to talk about Jesus. 'I believe all you tell me,' said the treasurer. 'Here's some water.

Can you baptise me now?' He got out of the chariot and Philip baptised him. Then the official drove home happily, longing to tell his friends in Ethiopia of his new faith.

Soon there were believers in nearly every town in Judea, Galilee and Samaria. In the port of Joppa, there lived a woman called Dorcas who liked to help poor people because she loved Jesus. One day she fell ill and died. When her friends heard, they asked Peter to come to Joppa.

As soon as he arrived a sad crowd of women showed him the clothes that Dorcas had sewn for them. Peter went up to the room where Dorcas lay. He knelt and prayed. Then he said to the dead woman, 'Dorcas, get up!' At once Dorcas opened her eyes and sat up. Peter helped her to her feet and called to her friends. The wonderful news spread all over Joppa, and many people believed in Jesus.

Everybody wanted Peter to tell them more about Jesus, so he agreed to stay on in Joppa. One day he went up to pray on the roof of the house where he was living. There God showed him in a dream a sheet coming down from the

sky, full of food. Peter felt pleased because he was hungry, but the food was the kind forbidden him by Jewish law. Then God told him that everything which he had made was good, and invited him to eat. Peter woke up. He was wondering what this dream meant when some men called to see him. They had been sent by a Roman officer, Cornelius, who wanted Peter to come to his house to tell him about Jesus. Jews were not allowed to mix with foreigners – but Peter remembered his dream. Now he understood that in God's eyes there were no differences between Jews and foreigners – God made them all, just as he had made different sorts of food. So Peter went with the men to meet the Roman officer.

Cornelius was delighted to see Peter. Although he was a Roman he loved and worshipped God. He led Peter into the house where his friends and relations were waiting to hear about God and his Son, too. 'God has shown me that he loves everyone, no matter what race they belong to,' said Peter. He started to tell them about Jesus.

While he was speaking the Holy Spirit filled the room and Cornelius and his friends found themselves praising God in other languages, just as the disciples had done in Jerusalem. The Jewish believers from Joppa were amazed, but Peter baptised Cornelius and his friends in the name of Jesus.

At home in Jerusalem life grew even more dangerous for the friends of Jesus. King Herod himself was helping the priests attack them. Fisherman James, who had left his boat years

before to follow Jesus, was killed, and Peter, back from Joppa, was arrested. He was closely guarded by four soldiers, but the followers of Jesus met together to pray for him, especially on the evening before his trial.

That same night Peter was sleeping chained between two guards. More soldiers guarded the gates. Suddenly a great light shone in his cell. An angel shook Peter awake. 'Get up at once!' The chains fell from Peter's wrists. He was free! Not

sure whether he was really awake or only dreaming, Peter followed the angel past the sleeping guards. The prison gate opened wide for them and they walked out. Peter found himself alone in the empty street. The cold air convinced him this was no dream. God had freed him! He ran to find his friends.

Hurriedly, Peter knocked at the house where many of his friends were still praying for him. 'Who is it?' called the servant girl, Rhoda. When she heard Peter's voice she told the others, but they simply could not believe her. 'It's true. He's still knocking!' cried Rhoda, who was so excited she had forgotten to let him in! Amazed, they opened the door and Peter came in. He told them how God had rescued him. Then he slipped away somewhere safe while his friends praised God and talked together about the wonderful things he was doing for them.